SEEKING GOD

OVER SEEKING THINGS

LESSONS IN PUTTING GOD FIRST

DANA DAVIS

Published by Dana Davis

Interior Formatting:
House Capacity Publishing
Support@housecapacity.com
www.housecapacity.com

Printed in the United States of America

ISBN-13: 978-1-955649-11-7

Contents

READER TESTIMONIALS

"I've known Dana since the 80's when he was just starting out as a professional drummer. I've watched Dana's gift open many doors for him. We have even had the opportunity to work together. When I look back on when I started as a young dude in the music world, I remember the challenges I encountered. They couldn't keep me down. I relied on God and overcame them. This book will help you face your shortcomings, both spiritually and naturally. You will see how when you follow God's direction, instead of trusting in your own ability, God will do exceedingly, abundantly, and above all, you could ever ask or think." – FRED HAMMOND

"When Dana first started touring with the Winans at the age of 16, he was just a big-headed little boy still growing into his body. Even at that young age, he was a phenomenal drummer. I've been fortunate to be able to call him a friend and brother, also proud of the man he has become. Dana is known around the world as an elite

musician with a lifetime of experiences. I am happy to see that he has put all of his knowledge and experiences in his new book SEEKING GOD OVER SEEKING THINGS is just that simple. This book will show you the importance of involving God in every decision you make. As Dana so often says, when God is your first and not your last resort, you will see Matthew 6:33 become a daily practice in your life." —*TIM BOWMAN*

"Dana and I toured with the Winans for many years in our 20's, traveling as roommates. He was the drummer and I was the road manager. This book chronicles his life as a multi-talented young musician who had access to lots of cash while absent of good money habits, disciplined spending, saving, and investing in the future.

Like any young man with popularity and cash, he was driven by the latest fashion, cars, and other activities that brought him affirmation in absence of his father who passed at an early age. He hopes to show others who they are and how to avoid the same mistakes through his authentic and transparent story." - *ERIK WILLIAMS*

ACKNOWLEDGEMENTS

I would like to thank God for this opportunity to share my story, and for putting the desire in me to accept this journey.

I would like to thank my awesome and lovely wife Anita and dedicate this book to her. Thank you for keeping my two boys occupied while I was working so hard to finish. Thank you for all of the times you would proofread my manuscript and encourage me to continue. It has been a long time coming but thanks to you, Anita, I was able to complete my first book.

To my sons Dana and Jacob, I dedicate this book to you both as well. You guys are amazing and funny, and so encouraging. Thank you for your kind words of love.

To all my friends (my homeboys). What an extraordinary bond we have built. I would not trade it for anything in this world. I really appreciate your honesty, transparency, and commitment to the brotherhood. Much love.

Thank you to my awesome extended family. There are too many of you to name. Throughout my life, you have all been very supportive.

I would like to thank my editor, Donna Robertson, for your professional input, advice, and commitment to helping me finish my book. Working with you has taught me so much more about writing. I'm truly grateful.

Thank you Rosetta Archer for helping me to name the chapters of this book.

Lastly, I would like to thank everyone who purchased this book. Because of your support, I will be able to help so many others through my testimony.

Special Thanks: R.I.H.

Willie Davis (my dad) 06/2/1932 – 2/21/1970

Geoffrey Davis (my brother) 4/17/1961 – 1/9/1997

LaunDale Lighten (my nephew) 4/26/1973 – 9/28/1999

Rogers Kimbrough (A.K.A. uncle Billy)
11/05/1930 – 4/1/2004

Charlie Jones (Grandpa A.K.A "Amen Jones")
12/28/1914 – 2/3/2008

Minnie Davis (my mom) 5/25/1932 – 8/29/2019

Foreword

I T HAS BEEN A PRIVILEGE to have been engaged in the maturation of the life of Dana Davis. I have had a front-row seat in all that the Lord has done for him. Over the years I have been connected to Dana in the roles of employer, encourager, mentor, brother, and friend. While having the pleasure of being connected in these various capacities, I have also been a cheerleader and a fan.

It is very satisfying to read the words that are penned, not only from his experiences, but also his heart. To see the younger brother of Willie and Geoffrey become a God-fearing man, husband and father is far beyond the words I can adequately express. To read the pages of this book is to follow a manual of spiritual growth. Living in a generation where *things* have become more important than education, community, and faith; it sparks a hope that our children can be brought back from the despair of their age, into the care of the Ancient of Days.

To every father or mother that has a child who seems to be straying from the path, read this book and find new inspiration that your prayers are not in vain.

Dana has shared with us that though we walk through the valley, we do not walk alone. *Seeking God Over Seeking Things* is a very digestible book, and before you know it, the writing will have taken you to the very end. This is a book that can be enjoyed over and over. As you read this book, you will have the same results as Dana—a fulfilled life by learning the lessons of making the right choices.

Because of Calvary,

Marvin L. Winans

INTRODUCTION

"But seek ye first the kingdom of God, and his right-eousness; and all these things shall be added unto you."
— *Matthew 6:33*

SEEKING GOD over seeking things. It sounds simple. It sounds like the right thing to do. So many times God has revealed this scripture to me, yet I ignored it. How great life would be if we would just take our eyes off of our circumstances and apply Matthew 6:33.

I was inspired to write this book for a number of reasons. One was to help someone see life through a different lens, and to see the danger of valuing things over family, friends, and purpose. Another reason was to give you a glimpse into my life from age 16 to adulthood, allowing you to see how reckless I once was with money, and prioritizing.

This book will also show you the dangers I put myself in because I chose to ignore sound wisdom. I rejected knowledge due to pride, stubbornness, low self-esteem, and bad influences. I was ungrateful and never satisfied with where I was or who I was in life. But what I learned is that time has a way of bringing you back full circle. You will either choose God's way, which brings you total fulfillment, or you will continue down the path you're on doing things with very little help from God.

I wrote this book to tell you my life story. Like me, you also have a life story, and after reading this book, I know that you will have a clearer understanding of the advantages of seeking God first. You will also become more aware of the disadvantages of seeking things first.

I pray that my testimony will be words of knowledge, wisdom, and encouragement for you and just a simple reminder of what God has told us to do.

1
FIRST THINGS FIRST

THROUGHOUT THE COURSE of my life, God has done more for me than I could ever do for myself. He blessed me with musical gifts and abilities that opened more doors for me than I could have ever imagined. Because of His favor, I have had some amazing life experiences and great opportunities that I would not have had otherwise.

My first break as a professional musician came when I was 16. Since that time, God has blessed me to work on awesome studio projects, write and produce songs, and travel the world working with renowned artists and musicians.

My career began as a drummer for the Winans. We toured all over Europe and other parts of the world, performing in front of massive audiences. The experience was incredible. It was my first time being exposed to different cultures and societies. God was doing something great in my life very early on, even opening the door for me to play drums for the Winans on the Arsenio Hall show.

I loved being able to travel the world as a musician. One of the most exciting things for me was going to L.A. for the first time. I remember how great it was meeting legendary music producer Quincy Jones and industry icons like Sheila E. I was excited to meet back up with "the king of the pocket" drummer Ricky Lawson. Opportunities were opening up for me everywhere. Before I knew it I was doing live recordings at Carnegie Hall and the Apollo Theater with The Winans. Later in my career, I also did a live recording with Byron Cage at the Apollo.

I met phenomenal gospel artists that I grew up listening to - Andrae Crouch,

The Hawkins family, and drummer Joel Smith. I traveled to Switzerland with Donnie McClurkin to play at the Montreux Jazz Fest, and worked on studio projects with producers like Billy Meadows, Cedric Caldwell, Eric Morgan, Mitchel Jones, Thomas Whitfield, Bishop Mike Brooks, PaJam, and Fred Hammond. I worked with Tim Bowman, Commissioned, J Moss, Thomas Whitfield, Aretha Franklin, and the list goes on.

God was opening many doors for me, and with all the opportunities I was given, including becoming a songwriter, one would think I should have been the happiest man in the world! But deep down inside, I felt like something was missing. I watched my musical abilities make room for me financially. Yet I complained, believing it just wasn't enough. Way deep in the back of my mind, I didn't feel I was as blessed as I should have been. Even though I may have appeared successful to others, I didn't feel successful. I compared myself to those around me, feeling as if I should be achieving on the same level as they were.

Instead of totally trusting God with my thoughts, needs, and desires, I found myself busy focusing on everyone and everything else. I wanted what they possessed, plus all they had achieved. I wanted their level of success so badly, that instead of thanking God for the amazing favor and generosity he had shown in my life, I became ashamed of the musical gifts and abilities God had given M.E.

Things were not moving fast enough for me. There I was, wanting more and more. My thoughts consisted of *How am I going to meet my needs? How am I going to achieve the things that I desire? And how do others perceive me?*

What a combination of fear and worry! I had no peace! No matter how much God was trying to do for me to get my attention, I allowed my independent attitude and complaining tendencies to prevent me from seeing all the things He was doing and had already done to bless me and provide for me.

One day, as I sat on my couch, frustrated and confused. I felt like God was asking me, "Why are you concerned with your needs - where you are going to live, or what people are thinking? Why are you worrying about your musical future?"

> "Therefore take no thought saying, what shall we eat? Or what shall we drink? Or wherewithal shall we be clothed? (For after all these things do the Gentiles seek) for your heavenly Father knows that ye have need of all these things, But seek ye first the kingdom of God, and his righteousness; and all these things shall be added unto you." – *Matthew 6:31-33 KJV*

What is God really trying to teach us? There are many illustrations in the bible that are similar to this scripture. The revelation I continue to get from these illustrations is that I must TRUST. In Exodus 16, God provided for Israel, because He wanted them to learn to trust Him. We, like the children of Israel, have to learn to trust Him.

Many would agree with me concerning Matthew 6:33, until it comes to the part about making God the first choice. For me, personally, God was always the last resort. Even when I did turn to God, I put Him on a time constraint.

Trusting in my own ability would always trump my dependence on God.

Over time, I began to see myself more clearly, realizing that I was filled with insecurities. As I began growing in my relationship with God and learning to obey His voice, I allowed him to reveal his wisdom.

I have learned that seeking after things first will only drive us to a place of wanting more things. That mindset will prevent us from ever being content or appreciative of what we already have. Making anything else a priority other than God is irrational thinking. Irrational thinking brings irrational decisions, and irrational decisions will always cause us to compromise. When we compromise, a lack of gratitude, patience, and trust will follow, and we will become fearful of the unknown.

2
ADJUST YOUR ATTITUDE

> *"Yea, though I walk through the valley of the shadow of death, I will fear no evil; for thou art with me; thy rod and thy staff they comfort me."*
> *— Psalm 23:4*

AFTER EXPERIENCING so much favor and blessing, there came a time when I was in a valley in my life. During this time, I was struggling with making the right decisions concerning my future. All the former excitement had died down. I was out of work and didn't know what my next steps should be.

You see, as a man, I'm used to being in control of my destiny. I had always relied on my own ability to get me what I needed. That was my level of comfort and dependency. However, I wanted different results this time.

During this season of my life, I was spending more of my time learning about God. I made the decision to practice what I had been preaching to others. Now mind you, I had many valleys where God tried to reveal Himself, but grasping what God was trying to show me was difficult because of where my focus and trust were during those times.

It never failed, whenever I thought it was taking too long for God to show up, I would begin to worry. Then I would start to reflect on my past, which led to me overthinking, responding irrationally, complaining, and not wanting to wait on God. I kept repeating the same tests and trials because of my decision not to wait. When you don't know which way to turn, and you discover what used to work is no longer working, it's easy for your brain to go tilt. The things I was seeing and hearing had me feeling some type of way! It was rough, and the old me was screaming, "Get me out of this mess!" I had a decision to make. It was either seek God or spend my time and energy worrying about it, which got me no-where. Worrying only made me more frustrated and impatient.

I started thinking about the story of the children of Israel and how they murmured and complained in the wilderness. As I revisited the story, I did a self-evaluation and saw things within myself that I saw in them. God was trying to take them to a place of promise, but instead of trusting God, they were always distracted by the things they saw on their way. They were so conditioned to being in bondage that it was hard for them to see themselves going into the promised land.

When you are in the valley, it's easy to look back at where you came from and compare it to where you are. If you are an impatient person, as I once was, you would prefer to go back to where you left off, because it's familiar territory. You would rather deal with the instability you had in that place. Even though things were not good where you were, you are willing to settle and go back because of the discomfort in the valley you're currently dealing with. But if you look carefully at Psalms 23:4, "Yea though I walk through the valley ..." the keyword is "THROUGH."

I always hear preachers say, when speaking to this part of the verse, "The scripture didn't say STAY there, it said go THROUGH." So that says to me, your length of days, or however long it takes you to go through the valley is determined by you. This is what I've learned in life, you can't get weary or annoyed when waiting on God. If you do, you're going to see time pass you by, and what should have taken a short period of time to get out of, is going to take a lot longer. Trust me, you don't want that! Don't let a trip that should have taken days to get you to your destination take years because of pride, doubt, unbelief, and fear.

Once I made the decision to stand down and surrender my will and my way to God, no matter where I was or what I was doing - whether I was at church, somewhere listening to music, watching television, or even talking with someone, I kept hearing Matthew 6:33.

> "Seek ye first the kingdom of God, and all these things shall be added unto you."

I would even see the same scripture on bumper stickers and billboards while driving. It reminded me of the insurance commercial about the duck and the man in a boat.

The man was trying to cover leaks in the boat, and every time he would cover one leak, another leak would happen. Now the whole time this is happening, the duck would call out the name of the insurance company - trying to get the man's attention because it knew the insurance company could solve the problem. Yet the man ignores the duck and continues trying to fix the problem on his own.

Now I have a question. Does the man in this story sound like you? I know he sounded like me. I had major issues with asking for help. As bad as I needed help, my pride, shamefulness, insecurities, and fear of what people would think or say, would not allow me to ask for help. I was just like the man in the commercial. Don't be like the man in the boat who ignored the voice of help, due to lack of respect for the messenger. God is always trying to get our attention. The question is, how long will it take? Will it take you watching your boat sink while you're in it, or will you get your ego out of the way and surrender to God? Please embrace the voice of God. He is saying, "Try me."

3
NO MORE FEAR

HERE IS ANOTHER part of Psalm 23 I've come to understand:

> v4 -*"Yea, though I walk through the valley of the shadow of death, I WILL FEAR NO EVIL."*

I will stop here because I want to speak to this part of the verse.

When you're in the valley, it appears as if everything evil is magnified!!! The things you experience in the valley can either make or break you. They can cause you to experience fear, or you can make a decision to fix your eyes on God. Some valleys have such a strong presence of evil, if you're not rooted and grounded in your faith, you can get caught up. Romans 10:17 says faith comes by hearing, and hearing by the word of God. You have to stay in God's word.

With fear as a distraction, it is easier for Satan to attempt to steal your joy, kill your faith, and destroy your hope. Fear can come on you fast! It will have you speaking negatively, and the more negative words you hear, the easier it becomes for you to not trust, nor wait on God.

I trusted God as long as things were going well for me, but the second I had to wait, "Hello fear." No more trusting God.

When you don't seek God first, you become fearful of leaving places, jobs, relationships, and positions when God is telling you to move. Being financially secure where you are will have you stuck and afraid to leave, but don't stay in that place - get out!!

Let me tell you a story about my Mom. Not only was she a strong woman, but she was also my

SHERO! In my family, there were nine of us - three boys and six girls. I am the youngest. My dad died when I was three years old. My mom unselfishly loved us so much that she sacrificed her needs as a woman companionship, financial security, emotional support, protection, and the balance that marriage brings, by making the decision to not remarry for the safety of her kids.

My hat is off to my Mom. I do not know of many women who would do that today. I have much respect for women who have had to carry the load all by themselves. Now that I am married, I understand the advantage and the importance of having both parents in the house, especially when you have kids. I thank God I have a wife whose values coincide with my values when it comes to raising a family. Let's go back to the story.

When my Dad died, my Mom had to hold it down for the family. She told me stories of how she would go to my dad's graveside, talk to God and grieve. When she pulled up to the house, she would get herself together, put her game face on, roll up her sleeves, and do what she had to do. You see, there was no time for crying when she got home. It was all about getting it done when it came to raising her nine kids. Now, can you imagine going through life stressing over the challenges you're facing, or having to walk through valleys while people are ridiculing you? How about the pressure of going to places for financial assistance and being rejected?

Imagine being the single head of the household while trying to keep things together. You're trying to stay upbeat, all the while fear is beating down your door. Fear is trying to fill your heart with the evil that it brings to your mind. With all the anxiety inside, you are still trying to do your best to keep from breaking down in front of your kids.

This part of the book is emotional for me. Now that I am a man, I understand all that she had to endure being a single parent. However, through it all, when it came to our needs, we never lacked. Yeah! We may not have gotten all the things that we desired, but she made sure we had what we needed. I am pleased to say that my mom was my example and my reality of what Matt 6:33 looks like in the flesh. With God by her side, she allowed Him to be the first and final stop when it came to her valleys. She made it through! It was not easy, but she made it through. Until the day that God called her home, he was her first choice, no matter what it looked like. No matter how she was feeling or what was being said, God was first.

There comes a time in life when you have to make a decision to be done with fear. You have to stop being afraid of rejection, failure, people, and all the evil that you encounter in the valley. Just like I did in my valley, you have to see God as being bigger than your circumstances. No matter what it looks like, what you're hearing, or how you feel, make the decision not to let fear trump the voice of God in the valley.

4
YOU WERE *ALWAYS* THERE

> *Psalm 23:4: Yea, though I walk through the valley of the shadow of death, I will fear no evil; for Thou Art With Me..."*

KNOW WE HAVE all had numerous *"but God"* moments in our lives. I'm sure everyone that is reading this book will agree with me, "If it had not been for the Lord who was with me ...." Pause and think about that for a moment!

When you're in the valley you're going to feel like you are in it all by yourself. But, it's comforting to know that God will never leave us nor forsake us. He is always with you.

Don't focus on the circumstances surrounding you. No matter what you are seeing or hearing, or even how you're feeling, just hold your peace. Watch what you say, and rest in knowing God is with you. In other words, put on your cool man walk while walking through your shadow of discomfort. Always remember, God is with you.

As I began to seek God, the scales started to fall off my eyes. Things became clearer to me. It was then that God was able to reveal things to me about myself. He also began revealing how he was with me. I think some valleys are orchestrated for our growth. Then there are valleys we create ourselves because of decisions we make. Decisions to hang out in places we should not, and with people that we should not allow into our lives. A side note: watch the people you surround yourself with. If they are not productive, progressing, or pushing you forward, get away from them. Or else, you will find yourself watching time pass you by.

I was once carjacked. It was all because I ignored the voice of God. The voice of God was telling me to leave where I was. God was giving me a window of opportunity to leave, but I ignored it. Being hard-headed could have cost me my life, *but God*! When I saw the guys run up on me, we all ran towards the car. [The car was the thing that could have cost me my life.] A guy then pumped the shotgun and pointed it at me. I knew that was my last day on earth, *but God*! In spite of my decision to stay and not leave when He told me to leave, the grace of God protected me. Trust me, I've gained a greater appreciation for God's voice and generosity. After that incident, and all of the others where God's grace intervened, oh yeah, it became a lot easier for me to recognize all the "*but God*" moments I had experienced in my life. God was with the children of Israel through all of their murmuring and complaining.

He is also with you and me. I started learning more about God's faithfulness through reading and hearing testimonies of others. I learned to go through the valley without fear. If I can give you one nugget, it would be to surround yourself with people who are transparent. It gets easier when you know the stories of others who trusted God in their valleys.

It became clearer and clearer to me that God was with me. Everything I needed was in His kingdom. If I would seek after righteousness, which meant doing things His way, I would not only be able to maintain while in the valley, but I could go through the valley without an ounce of fear or worry in my heart.

5
SOMETIMES THE TRUTH HURTS!

Here is the last part of this verse that I want to show you:

> *"Yea, though I walk through the valley of the shadow of death, I will fear no evil; for thou art with me; thy rod and thy staff they comfort me."*
> — *Psalm 23:4.*

In Psalm 23, the rod and staff both represent God's instruments of discipline and guidance. These were used by shepherds to guide the sheep, protect them, and keep them safe and in line. The rod and staff are also symbols of God's authority.

I made some bad choices in my life that cost me time, opportunities, money, friendships, jobs, and left me out of God's will. But thank God for His mercy and grace. He has always put me back where I belonged. Not only did God use His rod to discipline me, he used it to protect me from myself and from my enemies. God used His staff to guide me and pull me back whenever I started venturing off His path.

I believe God uses people to be a rod and staff. He places people in our lives to keep us out of harm's way and to keep us focused. We may not like it at first, but as time goes by, God gives us an opportunity to see and understand His generosity through those people. In the end, it causes us to have a heart of gratefulness toward Him and thankfulness for His love toward us.

The bible says a true friend sticks closer to you than a brother, and even though my big brother Willie aka "Junior" was vocal in my life, I also had friends who were like brothers. There were times as a young man when I was naive to things that could have hurt me, but because God never stopped trying to get my attention, he would use my friends to steer me in the right direction. They would have those harsh conversations with me. They never had a problem with telling me when I was wrong, or right. They never had a problem with agreeing or disagreeing. When it comes to God versus things, even to this day, they have no problem with getting me on the straight and narrow.

Here's one illustration - I was a negative person as a young man, so much so that I never saw the good in anyone. Yet my friend Chuck saw the good in everyone. Every time I would say something negative about someone, here comes God using my boy as a "ROD" to correct me.

When my mom was trying to teach me that I should be a good steward over what God blessed me with, I didn't want to hear the truth, but God was using her to try to show me wisdom and direction. He was using family, friends, and people of God to be a rod of correction and a staff to guide me. It is comforting to know that God places people in your life to show you His love, and to tell you the truth.

Being a father now, I can better relate to Psalm 23:4. Having children has made it so much easier for me to understand the bible. No matter what it looks like, my kids know that I am with them no matter what they are going through. They know they can call on daddy. I thank God for my kids. I always affirm them. I always show and tell my kids how much I love them. Because of that, they trust me.

- My kids may be afraid at first when facing challenges, but once they recognize that daddy is there with them, they are not afraid anymore. Even when I have to correct or discipline them, they may not like it then, but as time goes by, they understand that making the right decisions to obey daddy equals an abundance of blessings from dad. To me, what God wants is for us to trust Him and not be afraid, period! You're going to face challenges in your life. The valleys are coming, so fix your heart and mind and rest in knowing that God will be with you. He will provide, protect, and guide.

6
THE GREAT SPENDER

I WAS SIXTEEN when I started traveling around the world and making lots of money. Once I got a taste of making money, my nickname should have been The Great Spender. Back then, I had low self-esteem. Coming up in a family where I had older brothers, clothes didn't get thrown away. They got passed down from one brother to the next. Once I started making money, you can probably guess, in fact you already know what I was spending my money on. I would go to school with a pocket full of money. Whatever brand name clothes or shoes were popular at that time, I was wearing it. I did not save not one dime. My mom saw how reckless I was with my money - to the point that she said she was going to take my money away from me if I didn't slow down with the reckless spending. Instead of listening to her and embracing what she said, I got upset and told her I would quit working.

I was living with my Mom and not paying any rent. That was until she had enough of my careless spending and smart remarks, especially about quitting my job. Even after having to pay rent, it did not matter to me, because I was making tons of money for my age. I was addicted to money, food, and material things. Whatever I wanted, I got it, no matter the cost. When I look back at all of the money I made, sadly to say, I have nothing to show for it. All I have are memories of recklessness and costly financial lessons.

The Bible says, "Trust in the Lord with all of your heart and lean not to your own understanding. In all your ways acknowledge Him and He shall direct your path" (Prov. 3:5-6). Although I knew what to do, I found myself struggling with three things - trusting, praying, and reading the bible.

To get the results I needed, there had to be some discipline on my end. I was not conditioned to consistently trust, pray, or read the Bible. Even though I was taught, I had no desire, nor was I willing to commit to spending my time in this area. Reason being - I didn't know God. As a result, it was hard trusting and spending time with someone that I knew very little about. It was easier for me to do for myself, so I thought.

The lifestyle I had become accustomed to living without even knowing God, had led me to believe that I did not need Him. I had the ability to do whatever, get whatever, and work wherever, but the consequences of my thinking cost me dearly.

Better Backwards

As I got older, I became even more irresponsible. I had no discipline, and I did not pay my bills on time. I was in debt with credit cards and in tax trouble. I lived from check to check. My car was repossessed. Instead of investing in my future, which my mom, my sister Darlene who worked in the banking industry, and my employer, Bishop Winans had been trying to tell me, I was spending all my money on clothes, food, and hanging out. My favorite pastime was and still is roller skating!

Every time I went skating, I was buying something new to wear to impress the people who influenced me. Yeah, I spent thousands of dollars on clothes, only to ruin them by sweating them out. Now I'm going to expose you to one of my favorite food places - the gas station. When I went to the gas station, I did not just get gas. I would buy pop or juice, some chips, and a honey bun, every time. That didn't work out so well for me in the long run either.

Here's a funny story. I know you've heard the myth, you can tell where a person is from by the way they dress. I went to Hawaii with Ronald Winans back then to do a music workshop for the army's gospel choir, and during our leisure time we hung out at the beach. Sure enough, that myth became true. You see, from all the bad eating, I had gained a lot of weight. So, wearing swimming trunks with no T-shirt was not going to happen! I was extremely insecure.

I was at the beach walking in the water. In this particular area, you could see the fish because the water was so clear. Everybody there had on swimwear.

It was obvious that I was out of my element. I had on a silk, olive green short set with a perm in my hair! I know you're probably saying, "No you didn't", but yes I did.

I know it's hard to imagine me with hair because I don't have any hair now, but back then, I had hair. Go ahead and laugh. I admit it is funny! I thank God for two things: (1) that camera phones didn't exist in those days, and (2) social media sites did not exist like they do now. Had they existed, I know people would have plastered me all over social media.

I had no discipline when it came to food and spending money. My sister was always trying to help me. I mean she was going on and on about me "saving my money." My quest for things was louder than the voice of financial discipline. I was able to come and go as I pleased. I was able to buy what I wanted. I was getting tons of work, so who needed God?

I had money to get me things at that time, ignoring the fact that I was getting older. I paid no attention to a true statement, "All good things come to an end." The season that I was in was slowing down and coming to an end. Back then, I didn't live for tomorrow. I lived for the moment. I couldn't hear what the wise council was saying. It wasn't making sense. You see, things validated me and brought me prestige. As long as I had money in my pockets and new clothes on, I had confidence. When my clothes got old and the money ran out, my insecurity came back.

You are not your things!

No matter how much my friends and family would do and say, trying to get me to see my worth as a person, all I could see was the feeling I got when my peers would look at me and compliment me. That was the ultimate high for me! My quest for validation based on the things I had acquired taught me that time has a way of bringing you back full circle, and God will be right there waiting. After the cares and burdens of this life have weighed you down... After they have driven you to a place of being desperate and not knowing which way to turn, God will be right there waiting - not judging, but showing you His love.

I learned the hard way that trying to live this life without God will cost you so much. Yeah, you will experience some good times and even enjoy fulfilling some pleasures of life that you created, but it will never equal, nor surpass the things that God has for you. God will bless you, provide for you, protect you, and give you favor, but why stop there when you can have a trusted relationship with a God who will not only supply all of your needs, He will give you the desires of your heart and steer you in the right direction.

7
TESTED AND TRIED! GOD CAN BE TRUSTED

G OD WAS TRYING to get the children of Israel to trust Him throughout the entire process. Through all the supernatural signs and miracles
that were displayed the *"but God"* moments - their
mental bondage kept them enslaved to their past.
You have to ask yourself these questions, "Am I enslaved to my past?" Do my past failures, disappointments, hurts, scars, insecurities, and agony of defeat
keep me mentally bound?"

God used Moses to try to get them to see Him.
However, because of the lifestyle of bondage they
were accustomed to living, they missed out on going

to the land that was promised to them. They were fearful of the unknown. They were complainers and they were full of ungratefulness. Not only did they miss out on going to the promised land, but Moses missed out, too!

Moses' frustration with the people made him act out against God, which cost him big time. It's not that they didn't recognize God's power and love, but the weight of their past was too heavy for them to rise above what they were seeing, hearing, and feeling. I believe that grieved God to the point that he no longer desired to do anything more to prove Himself to them.

What I got from this story is that God loves hard. To the point that He goes all out to try to convince you that He is all you will ever need. All He wants in return is a trusted relationship.

His word says, "...Yea, I have loved thee with an everlasting love: therefore with lovingkindness have I drawn thee."
— *Jeremiah 31:3*

But when you show Him your ungratefulness, continual complaints, and disbelief in Him, you tie His hands. You know He is real, and you've seen His hand in your life, but your head keeps getting in the way. Your trust in your own ability continues to keep you enslaved to your past, so the path to your promising future remains cloudy.

I was that person. God waited until I was ready. I wasted time going in a circle looking at what was for me. But I couldn't have it until I was willing to let God be God. I'm so glad God didn't move on and let me die in my wilderness of ungratefulness, murmuring, and complaining. I'm grateful that He gave me another chance.

> "Be careful (anxious) for nothing; but in every thing by prayer and supplication with thanksgiving let your requests be made known unto God. 7 And the peace of God, which passeth all understanding, shall keep your hearts and minds through Christ Jesus.
>
> 8 Finally, brethren, whatsoever things are true, whatsoever things are honest,

whatsoever things are just, whatsoever things are pure, whatsoever things are lovely, whatsoever things are of good report; if there be any virtue, and if there be any praise, think on these things."

—*Phillipians 4:6-8*

8
GIANTS IN THE PROMISED LAND

WHEN YOU SEEK GOD FOR your needs, dreams, desires, and purpose in life, there are going to be giants. They may be so big, tall, and wide, that they will make you want to stay where you are. But look at the giants as an opportunity to experience a *"but God"* moment.

God told Moses that He had a place for them. It was a place with everything they would ever need or desire. Moses sent out twelve men to check out the land. Some of the men brought back a message of fear concerning the giants saying, "Yeah we saw the land and it's everything God said, but there are some giants." But Caleb, being one of the twelve spies, said "so what, with God on our side, we can take the giants and possess the land!" Clearly, we can see the difference between those who were still in bondage to their past, versus those who were free from that bondage.

David had the same attitude of confidence when he took on Goliath. Again, we see in this story how God wanted to bless Israel and give them victory, but for a long time they were letting a giant stand in the way. The soldiers weren't seeking God for answers on how to get to the place of victory. They just remained on the battlefield, running from the giant every time he showed up - that is until David came along and said 'I'm not afraid to take on this giant!'

What made David and Caleb's language different was their experience and their relationship with God. They knew what they were capable of with God in their corner. They knew they could go to God and get all the power they needed to deal with any situation that was standing in front of them. Seeking God first puts us in a position of trusting God based on the knowledge we have of him.

All my failures and bad decision making was tied to my lack of knowledge and relationship with God. There's a difference in knowing God exists and having a true relationship with Him.

What giants have kept you from moving forward? How many opportunities have passed you by because of people? How much time have you wasted because of fear? How many opportunities have you lost because of your own recklessness with your money? What giants do you need to conquer by God's power? Had Moses listened and kept himself surrounded with positive people, maybe it would not have been so easy for him to lose focus.

As I reflect back over my life, I'm seeing how I could have avoided many of life's hard knock lessons had I only listened to the people God placed in my life. If I had placed my trust in him instead of trusting in my own ability, it would have saved me a lot of time and unnecessary frustration.

9
KEYS TO THE GOOD-LIFE

WITH ALL THE BUMPS and bruises we encounter from bad decisions, life has a way of showing us the value of God, family, friends, and things—in that order.

In life, things should be last on the list.

When things are at the top of your list, know that you will always be deaf to the voice of reason. You will always chase after those things. You will never be satisfied or content with what you have. You will always be frustrated when you have to wait. Know that you will always be dishonest with yourself, even when trying to justify your need for things. You have to free yourself from the bondage of things that keep you from moving forward. You have to get to a place where you have control over things and not allow things to have control over you. If you don't, you will never see God as the end all and be all for every situation, good or bad. God should be first! I cannot say it enough.

I thank God for his grace and mercy. Thinking back on how patient God was with me during all my years of bad decision-making really helped me to see God's love for us. Instead of allowing me to be destroyed by stubbornness and disobedience, He allowed me to grow, and to learn how to trust in Him and seek first the kingdom. As He says in His Word, when we seek first the kingdom of God and His righteousness, all the things will be added to us. Seeking God first is saying "I trust you." Seeking Him means humbling yourself and being willing to wait on what God says.

Our lives can change for the better when we make a decision to do things God's way. I have learned to allow God to lead and guide me with his ability.

Over time, God used my sister to show me how to manage my money.

Learning to be a good steward and to appreciate what God has blessed me with has made a big difference in my life.

Seek God first and do not let your ego get in the way. Do not let the pressures of this world cloud your vision! Let God surround you with people who will tell you the truth whether you want to hear it or not. He will use those people to help take you into that promised land where all your needs will be met.

"But thou shalt remember the LORD thy God: for it is he that giveth thee power to get wealth, that he may establish his covenant which he sware unto thy fathers, as it is this day."

— *Deuteronomy 8:18*

"And the Lord will make you the head and not the tail; you shall be above only, and shall not be beneath, if you heed the commandments of the Lord your God, which I command you today, and are careful to observe them. So you shall not turn aside from any of the words which I command you this day, to the right or the left, to go after other gods to serve them."

— *Deuteronomy 28:13-14*

"I wait for the Lord, my soul doth wait, and in his word do I hope

— *Psalm 130:5"*

It is true that good things come to those who wait on the Lord. Put your trust in Him. Fill yourself with knowledge and the wisdom of God. When you do that, it will not be hard to rise above those things and times in life that bring discomfort.

Remember this, things don't make you, fear breaks you, and worrying keeps you faithless.

Let me leave you with these keys to having a balanced life.

Having faith in God = Trust.

Having a relationship with God = Prayer.

Having knowledge of who God is = Reading.

For me, there is no plan "B". God is the end all and be all to my existence.

When it comes to your past, present, and your future, I encourage you to let Matthew 6:33 be the foundation to every decision that you'll ever have to make in your life.

APPENDIX
My Financial Check-list

I F I HAD FOLLOWED this process when I was younger, I would've avoided many disappointments. Here's the financial plan my sister Darlene Boswell (over 45 years in banking), helped me to put in place. This checklist was very helpful to me; however, things didn't change overnight, I had to patiently work through the process.

If you don't have a financial plan in place, feel free to use my checklist to get started.

DO's and Don'ts:

Do understand how to manage the money you make.

Pay your bills

Save for Life-events*

Have an Emergency Savings (3-6 months of expenses) Plan for the future you want**

- Life-events*
- Marriage
- Arrival of Children
- Job Change
- Illness
- Retirement

Anticipate and 'save' for events that may impact your income earning ability. For example, as a musician it is important that I have reliable transportation to get back and forth to Gigs. I need to make sure I have savings to take care of routine maintenance, repairs, or vehicle replacement. It is crucial that I have my own resources (music equipment, technology, etc.).

Don't count money until it is in your hands.

Why?So often we spend our money before we have it in our hands! When you use this method, you're playing Russian roulette. This is a dangerous way to manage your money and it is certainly not worth the heartache you will experience. Gigs are like a concert set list; things are subject to change. This is the reason you should ONLY count the money that you have Saved, and not the money you're expecting to receive!

How I distribute the money I get:

Give 10% tithes out of every check

Give offering(s) out of every check

Set aside money for Emergency Savings (3-6 months Expenses)

Set aside money for Life Events Savings

Set aside money for taxes (most gigs will not take taxes out)

Set aside money for mortgage (or renter's) insurance

Set aside money for car insurance

Set aside money for health insurance

Set aside money for life insurance

Set aside money for retirement

Set aside money for music equipment (Career)

I suggest that you get with someone that you trust to help you understand where you are financially.

Made in the USA
Columbia, SC
20 February 2022

56301458R00040